99 words

collected by Liz Gray

DARTON · LONGMAN + TODD

First published in Great Britain in 2011 by
Darton, Longman and Todd Ltd
1 Spencer Court
140-142 Wandsworth High Street
London
SW18 4JJ

ISBN 978-0-232-52889-3

A catalogue record for this book is available from
the British Library.

Designed by Crescent Lodge Design Ltd
Printed and bound in Malta by Gutenberg Press Ltd

PREFACE

If you had breath for no more than 99 words,
what would they be?

It was this question which came to mind when
a whiplash injury left me suddenly unable to read
or write comfortably, sometimes to talk, for more than
a few minutes. My hectic schedule making television
documentaries stopped short and I found myself
entering a strange period of enforced retreat.
Words began to seem extraordinarily precious.

The effects of the injury crystallized a disillusion
I was already beginning to feel before it happened,
a weariness with the volume and speed of unwanted
incoming messages – spam, junk, spin, empty
promises. I could hear Robert Wyatt:

'We get so out of touch
Words take the place of meaning.'

Once on a filming trip to South Africa I went down
with a high fever. Alone in the hotel room I felt miles
from home and fearful. On a long-distance call, my friend
Harry Underhill suggested that I imagine inviting anyone
I felt could help. The imagined group that gathered in
my room that night got me through until the fever
subsided next morning.

On this long-haul recovery I began thinking about
the voices I love – writers, artists, musicians and thinkers
who choose words with the greatest of care because they
know their value can be limitless. On bad days, particularly,
I tried to imagine whose voice I would most want to hear.

Before all this, I had made films about the art and history
of Islam. It came back to me now that, according to the
Qu'ran, the Creator – and all of creation – can be expressed
in 99 names. Maybe 99 words could be enough?

Slowly the question formed itself: If you had breath for no more than 99 words, what would they be? The suggestion of last words was not intended to be morbid but rather a device for choosing 99 essential words. For symmetry I decided to collect 99 responses.

I thought this would take maybe a year or so and fill the time until I had recovered enough to go back to work. A few months after I began, however, it emerged that I have a rare genetic condition underlying and exacerbating the effects of the injury. The question became more significant to me – reading and working onscreen are as difficult now as when I started.

Working without a deadline then has been a necessity for me – and for many contributors too. I know this request presented something of a challenge. Nevertheless the responses arrived: letters, faxes, emails, phone calls, sometimes months after I sent my question and often with an uncanny sense of timing. Invariably their 99 words were exactly what I needed to hear at that moment. Unexpected latecomers brought the total to 101 and two people working with contributors gave their words too.

Nelson Mandela was one of the first I approached in 2004. I was given a free hand to choose his words, provided they would not be used for profit. Scilla Elworthy had just set up Peace Direct, a British charity supporting and publicising conflict resolution worldwide – a process built on the power of words. Thanks to the generosity of all the contributors and to the efforts of Brendan Walsh and the team at DLT, the royalties of 99 pence from the sale of each book will go to Peace Direct.

Seven years later, the collection is complete. If not for the patient collaboration and tireless support in every way of Janice Gardner, it might have taken another seven. I'm immensely grateful to her, to Claire de Boursac and Miriam Wandless for their onscreen work and to Margaret Busby for her encouragement, especially at the start. I would also like to thank the friends, family and neighbours who have given their time to help me contact contributors and translate their words.

The requesting and receiving of pieces has been a lifeline for me during a time of great change and uncertainty. Each arrival has been an unexpected birthday. This is a very personal anthology, but at the same time I'm hoping that the book will be a gift for anyone else who finds themselves, for whatever reason, lost for the words they need.

99 words is dedicated to the memory of those contributors who didn't live to see it finished: Adrian Mitchell, Nuala O'Faolain and Kazuo Ohno.

Liz Gray

I dreamed I was in a distant world. There was an object on my palm. It was sky blue and speckled and shaped strangely like a human head. Within it, I was told, there is a sticky liquid, which will coagulate to form a creature, which will peck its way out, spread its wings and leap into the sky. I laughed at the impossibility of such a thing. Then I woke and stepped into the sunlight. I stretched my arms and let the birdsong enter me. I knew that the distant world was this world and I was glad.

99

David Almond
novelist and storyteller

AUTORRETRATO A LOS CINCUENTA Y CUATRO AÑOS

Soy Homero Aridjis,
nací en Contepec, Michoacán,
tengo cincuenta y cuatro años,
esposa y dos hijas.

En el comedor de mi casa
tuve mis primeros amores:
Dickens, Cervantes, Shakespeare
y el otro Homero.

Un domingo en la tarde,
Frankenstein salió del cine
    del pueblo
y a la orilla de un arroyo
le dio la mano a un niño,
    que era yo.

El Prometeo formado con
    retazos humanos
siguió su camino, pero desde
    entonces,
por ese encuentro con el monstruo,
el verbo y el horror son míos.

SELF PORTRAIT AT FIFTY FOUR YEARS OLD

I am Homero Aridjis,
I was born in Contepec, Michoacán,
I am fifty-four,
with a wife and two daughters.

In the dining room of my house
I had my first loves:
Dickens, Cervantes, Shakespeare
and the other Homero.

One Sunday afternoon
Frankenstein came out of the town movie
house and on a stream's bank
held out his hand to a boy, who was me.

The Prometheus pieced out of
    human remnants
went on his way, but since then,
out of that encounter with the monster,
the verb and the horror are mine.

translation by George McWhirter

Homero Aridjis
poet, co-founder Grupo de los Cien (100 Artists for the Environment)

'Being there' for the birth of my first grandchild has been, to me, just as momentous as 'being there' in the pursuit of a humane and substantive peace for a nation long held captive by a ruthless military occupation. The space that unites the personal and the collective, the private and the public, is one in which artificial boundaries collapse and the affirmation of life and human dignity gain meaning. Peace has to be just as tangible as a new-born, just as fragile, and yet just as breath-taking in its promise. To be there is the true miracle.

Hanan Ashrawi
founder MIFTAH, the Palestinian Initiative for the
Promotion of Global Dialogue and Democracy

Those who think life must be meaningless to people
who can't believe in a god are mistaken. Knowing
one is not equipped to perceive life's meaning
is not the same as feeling it to be meaningless.
Twenty words from a poem by a man who is
certainly religious – from *The Rite* by Czeslaw Milosz –
mean a great deal to irreligious me:

'Perhaps we should begin by worshipping a stone,
An ordinary fieldstone, its very being.
And pray without opening our lips.'

Diana Athill
writer and former editorial director, André Deutsch

Me inicié en la vida inventándome sueños y personajes… El tiempo los decantó dejándome lo esencial. Como un árbol, sé cuál es el fruto que debo dar, pero sé también que sólo el tiempo dejara sentir cuál será mi mejor y más dulce fruto… Hoy encontré un viejo músico, fuerte como un árbol y pegado a la tierra. Me entregó la mejor melodia que maduró con sus años; me enseñó que mi música debe perdurar… que tenga los sonidos y las palabras de los otros y las mías. Con ellas quiero caminar, sembrar espíritu y alegría para dar…

I started in life inventing dreams and characters… Time filtered them to leave me the essential. Like a tree, I know which fruits I am to bear; I also know that only time will reveal which is to become my best and sweetest… Today I met an old musician, strong as a tree and as grounded; he gave me his best melody, ripened with his years; he taught me that my music must last, that it holds the sounds and the words of others as well as mine. I'll travel with them, sowing my spirit and spreading my happiness…

99

Susana Baca
singer, champion of Afro-Peruvian music

People often ask me why I have spent most of
my life concerned with the consequences of
conflict and violence. The simple answer is, why not?

The honest answer is difficult. It is about the
suffering of refugees. It is about the short life
of compassion, how quickly it is born and how
quickly it dies. It is about the stranger to whom
we owe nothing. It is how our society will be
judged and how we discover our humanity.
It is finding our reward through the eyes of
those to whom we owe nothing. It is about love.

Helen Bamber
co-founding director Helen Bamber Foundation
working with survivors of conflict and violence

Every war has happened
because of some disagreement
about *names*.

It's such an unnecessary foolishness,
because just beyond the arguing
there's a long table of companionship,
set and waiting for us to sit down.

What is praised is one, so the praise is one too,
many jugs being poured into a huge basin.
All religions, all this singing, one song.

Sunlight looks different on this wall
than it does on that wall,
but it is still one light.

We have borrowed these clothes,
these time-and-space personalities,
from a light, and when we praise,
we are pouring them back in.

Rumi, translated by Coleman Barks

Coleman Barks
poet and translator of Rumi

An open heart
can become more spacious.
Where is the key
to a closed one?

Grasping is futile.
Rejecting is painful.
Care lightly and gently,
like a mother holding a child,
not too loose, not too tight.

We have the gift of awareness. Creative awareness
wakes us up to life and its possibilities. Its main
qualities are acceptance and creative engagement.
We accept things as they are, thus grounding
ourselves in the moment. We creatively engage
with difficulties by understanding the inner
and outer conditions that created them and by
choosing to be spacious and open in this moment.

Martine Batchelor
meditation teacher and writer

Don't forget that what is happening now is a
mystery. Then notice how strong is the habit
to ignore this. Those views and opinions that
seize your attention are poor substitutes for the
overwhelming weirdness of life. Ask yourself,
softly but sincerely, 'What is this?' Then wait
in the silent, pregnant unknowing that follows.
Don't expect anything to happen. Discard even
your most treasured beliefs. Allow the questioning
to take hold until it suffuses body and mind.
Let yourself be surprised again by ordinary things.
Then respond to this moment in ways you would
not have thought possible.

Stephen Batchelor
lecturer, meditation teacher and writer

Words from the mouths of people who carry hate are received like daggers, more painful than the sharpness of a knife.

Words can devastate, abandoning you to humiliation worse than death.

Imagine being a child and suffering the blows coming from the fists and the mouths of the very people who are supposed to cherish you. The physical abuse is betrayal enough; the verbal abuse remains like an inescapable toxic companion.

Words can also ease the pain, soothing like a balm with their kindness. A compassionate and thoughtful voice can reclaim the isolated child with tender sounds, delicately loving.

Camila Batmanghelidjh
founder and leader Kids Company and The Place 2Be

Richard Rumbold, a Republican executed
in June 1685 at the Gallows Market Cross
in Edinburgh – hanged, drawn and quartered
after the Monmouth Rebellion, said this on
the scaffold:

'I am sure there was no man born marked of
God above another; for none comes into the
world with a saddle on his back, neither any
booted and spurred to ride him.'

Tony Benn
former Labour MP and Cabinet Minister

I am enclosing an extract from my
Valedictory Speech as Speaker of the
House of Commons, 26 July 2000.

I have not had a boring day in my working life
and, for that, I am grateful to all of you.

I say to you, rejoice in your inheritance,
defend your rights and remember always that
the privileges the House enjoys were dearly won
and must never be squandered. You elected me
in the springtime, and I shall retire in the autumn,
which marks a fitting seasonal conclusion to my
period in office. Therefore I say to you all, in a
phrase that you all know so well, but which has
never been more true than now, 'Time's Up'.

99

Betty Boothroyd
Baroness Boothroyd, OM, PC, first woman speaker of the House of Commons

When there seems only the memory of warmth
and the music of remembering, still time to seek
the feel of colour and the smell of words and the
jubilation of silence and the sweet taste of sound,
the mysterious rhythm of blood and friendship
that we know creates, sustains, uplifts, the surprise
of what lingers, survives, grows when we are ash,
the soulfulness of hope, the magic of the sun,
the promise of the night, those stubborn, patient
tremors of ecstasy and belief: and love and love and
love and love and love and love and love love love

Margaret Busby
writer and publisher

God holds the world in his hands.

He is not a bystander
at the pain of the world
but is there, in the dock, on the rack,
high on the gallows tree.

Through him,
our pain and prayer are somehow
used in the divine economy.

The blood shed in Salvador
will irrigate the heart of some financier
a million miles away,
while the terror, pain, and despair
of people swamped by lava, flood or earthquake
will be caught up like mist
and fall again,
a gentle rain on arid hearts or souls despairing
in the back streets of Brooklyn.

Sheila Cassidy
hospice medical director, advocate for human rights and victims of torture

The sight of new life stirs the heart. No matter how low we feel, tumbling puppies, tiny pink piglets – even the soft furry buds of willow melt away stress and strain. For me it is the birth of a new plant. To find new roots emerging from the base of a cut stem still stirs my soul – the same with seedlings.

Take a few beans or peas, put them in a glass jar half-filled with damp paper, stand it in a warm room. First a root then a growth shoots. You watch new life. The soul responds.

Beth Chatto
plants-woman, gardener and writer

BIRTH

After the snow, the wind, the rain,
comes spring. Blackbirds nest again.
Kites circle the Clettwr for blood.
Skylarks spiral into measureless blue.
These are the blood-days. After flood,
the breaking waters, a single ewe
in the field corner treads the earth,
turning and turning in her nest of pain,
absorbed and passionate for the birth
of what she can't believe in yet or name,
but knows it instantly, her lamb
washed in a storm from the cave of her womb,
its cry, its smell like the sea, she wild
with love as human mother for her child.

Gillian Clarke
National Poet of Wales,
co-founder and president Ty Newydd, the Welsh Writers' Centre

From the water of Mary or from the blowing of Gabriel,
In the image of Man existent from mud,
The Spirit immanenced in the person which is cleansed
From nature, which you name by 'prison' (sijîn).
Due to this his abiding was lengthened,
Therein more than a thousand years appointed,
Spirit from God and no other, and because of that
He revived the dead and built a bird from mud
So that it be true for him that his origin is from his Lord
And by it have effect in the high and in the low.

95   An extract from the chapter *The Wisdom of Elevation in the Word of Jesus* taken from Ismail Hakki Bursevi's translation of and commentary on *Fusus al-Hikam* by Muhyiddin Ibn 'Arabi, rendered into English by Bulent Rauf.

Grenville Collins
chairman, Ibn 'Arabi Society

FORTY-SEVEN WORDS (FOR LM)

Thanks for putting up with me.
The best years were with you –
So kind, and such good company.
Thanks for putting up with me.
By loving me, you helped me be
A loving person too.
Thanks for putting up with me.
Best thing of all was you.

47

Wendy Cope
poet

Love, compassion, kindness, interdependence, truth,
goodness. Beauty, harmony integrity integrality
forbearance, patience, understanding, light,
rain flowers trees soil birds, animals insects
people togetherness, unity, sound, music orchestration
dance, walking talking thinking pondering concentrating
sameness otherness health happiness breath water
air earth and sunlight moonlight, stars rainbow
mountains lakes rivers birdsong prayer meditation

'More than you need will always be greed.'

Silence quietness peace inspiration bliss. Work
diligence craft application agreement, writing
singing painting drawing composing digging
gardening, food vegetables fruit nuts seeds
communicating carefully. Life, looking seeing
understanding teaching making drawing reading
arranging cooking eating, bathing relieving
Family. Peace.

99   This is the only way I could choose 99 words.
It makes up my world – more or less. Sorry it
is not a 'text' or a 'story' but it is the only way
I could compress myself into 99 words. One
sentence in the middle came to me yesterday
whilst talking to my taxi driver – I hope you
like it.

Keith Critchlow
painter, teacher, designer and writer

'To see a world in a grain of sand,
And to see heaven in a wild flower,
Hold infinity in the palm of your hand
And eternity in an hour.'

William Blake

'However much you study, you cannot know
without action. A donkey laden with books is
neither an intellectual nor a wise man. Empty of
essence what learning has he, whether upon his
back he carries books or firewood?'

Sheikh Sa'adi of Shiraz

67

William Dalrymple
travel writer and historian

BODY AND SPIRIT

How can a world be contained in clay,
or the sky fit beneath the earth?
Never, by God! You're beyond this world
even during this life, in this very moment.
A bird flies above in unknown skies,
its shadow cast upon the earth.
The shadow of the shadow of the shadow
of the heart… is what the body is.
How can the body reach the heart's level?
A man sleeps, his spirit is like the sun
shining in the sky while he's in pajamas.
Spirit lies concealed in shrouded absence
and the body tosses and turns under a blanket.

Rumi, translated by Robert A H Darr

Robert Abdul Hayy Darr
writer and interpreter of Afghan literature and culture,
follower of Sufi poet Raz Mohammed Zaray

99 words are too many for my last breath, but not for this one.

In Europe where average families barely reach two children, increasing numbers of young women and men will freeze their eggs and sperm and then get sterilized, thus making 'conception' rather than 'contraception' the future leitmotif of reproductive behaviour. When a couple desires a child, they will resort to in vitro fertilization. And since a planned child is both wanted and loved, will such separation of sex ('in bed') and reproduction ('under the microscope') not strengthen rather than weaken the future nuclear family?

Dream or nightmare?

Carl Djerassi
chemist, developer of the oral contraceptive pill, novelist and playwright

These are the last words ever written under the sun, ever uttered,
the last words because there is no one left to hear them, read them.
Only the dead in the darkness of the past.

Was it worth it?

Each of you tell me before the stars and the sun blacken out.

Was it worth it?

Was there enough love for all the pain?

Enough green for all the tears?

Enough you and me and the child?

Only now can we ask and wonder if we were patient enough,
worthy enough, under the sun as it dies of love.

Ariel Dorfman
novelist, poet, playwright, human rights activist

To Amy, with love

THE GUEST HOUSE

This being human is a guest house.
Every morning a new arrival.

A joy, a depression, a meanness,
some momentary awareness comes
as an unexpected visitor.

Welcome and entertain them all!
Even if they're a crowd of sorrows,
who violently sweep your house
empty of its furniture,
still, treat each guest honorably.
He may be clearing you out
for some new delight.

The dark thought, the shame, the malice,
meet them at the door laughing,
and invite them in.

Be grateful for whoever comes,
because each has been sent
as a guide from beyond.

Rumi, translated by Coleman Barks

Gill Doust
psychotherapist

'In a hedgeless country of high downland, on a road that came flowing down, a long white ribbon, straight as it were out of the eastern sky, we would watch, each succeeding spring, for the first appearance of the fairy cruisers of the road.'

Kenneth Grahame, from his introduction to Sanger's *Seventy Years a Showman*

Apart from the sheer beauty of this sentence there is a certain appropriateness about it as 'Lord' George Sanger was one of the founders of the Showmen's Guild and was its second-ever president, serving from 1900 to 1908. It is the most evocative description of the arrival of the fair I have ever come across.

Graham Downie
fairground historian

Our senses vary. For instance, my ears might
not be attuned as yours, and your eyes might
take more light. The contrasts may be slight,
but imagine each of your senses differed from
mine and we could 'feel' divergently about an
identical experience. Consider now seven billion
people, their combination of senses unique,
each 'feeling' our planet differently, and you'll
find there as many worlds as there are people.
Try to heed the views of others, you might have
missed a thing or two, and if given the chance,
share your world, no one sees it as you do.

Inua Ellams
performance poet, graphic artist and designer

If I look back I see
that fear lies to me.

'You'll fail,' it said to me when I started out on the path.
'Here's how,' painting detailed pictures of pain.
When I was on the way fear scared me again and again
'Too weak, too old, turn back.'

I did walk on, encumbered by this load.
It wasn't easy,
but it wasn't what I'd been told.

I didn't fail.
Without the load I might have stumbled less.

The trick is to hear
when it is fear speaking
and hear it fast enough to let it drop.

Scilla Elworthy
peace and human rights activist,
founder Oxford Research Group and Peace Direct

Un savant offrit au Sultan
ses réflexions en 99 volumes.
Pensant que la vie n'y suffirait
point, le Sultan lui accorda 99
mois pour en faire un résumé de
9 volumes.

Le savant revint. Le Sultan
impatient lui ordonna de
résumer plus encore: 99 mots en
99 semaines.

Le jour venu, le Sultan admiratif
déclara: "Tu as su réduire
tes réflexions en 99 mots. Je
t'accorde 99 jours. Fais-le donc
en une seule phrase."

Finalement le Sultan lut: "Dieu
est un, Muhammad est son
serviteur et son messager."

A wise man gave the Sultan 99
volumes of wisdom. Thinking he
would never find time to read
them, the Sultan gave the man
99 months to write a 9-volume
summary.

When he returned, the impatient
Sultan ordered him to reduce it
again – 99 words in 99 weeks.

The Sultan was impressed by
the man's work. When he
returned he told him: 'You've
reduced it to 99 words. Now
take 99 days and come back
with just one sentence.'

The day came and the Sultan
read: 'There is no God but Allah
and Muhammad is his Prophet.'

99

91

Kudsi Erguner
Sufi musician, ney flute player

S'IL NE ME RESTAIT QUE 99 MOTS A DIRE

Je dirais que ma vie n'a été qu'un voyage
Dans l'immensité du monde
Et la labyrinthe des livres
Où j'ai récolté au hasard
Du vent de l'imaginaire
Ces précieux diamants
Que sont les mots
A chaque fois voleur
De coeur et de sentiment
Et chemin faisant
Le pas au vent d'ivresse
J'ai dessiné sur le papier blanc
La silhouette fugitive de mes rêves
Avant de disparaître
A l'heure où les livres se ferment
Posant ma vie fragile
Sur l'horizon du roman
Ne prenant, en somme
Que le temps de mourir.

IF I SHOULD HAVE ONLY 99 WORDS LEFT TO SAY

I would say that my life has
    been but a journey
In the world's immensity
And the maze of books
Where at random I have
    gathered
These precious diamonds
Words are
Every time a thief
Of heart and feelings
And making my way
Stepping in the wind of euphoria
I have drawn on the white paper
The fleeting outline of my
    dreams
Before disappearing
At the time of closing of the
    books
Laying my brittle life
On the novel's horizon
Only taking, in sum
The time to die.

translation by
Stéphane Cornicard

98

Maxence Fermine
writer and poet

Chekhov said, 'My religion is kindness.'

Julia Kristeva said you only have to look at the faces of strangers to understand the absolute non-existence of banality in all human beings.

The Chinese word 'shi' has 73 different meanings depending on how it's pronounced: you can construct the sentence, 'The master is fond of licking lion spittle' just by saying the word 'shi' over and over again.

My brother struck a match and the whole box caught fire: he stood motionless with this dense white flare in his fingers, as if he were holding a new star in his hands.

William Fiennes
writer and founding director First Story, creative literacy charity

The decision seems quite simple, keep walking or turn back. Apart from the slight heat haze, the road ahead looks clear to me.

Still I hesitate.

All is quiet, maybe too quiet.

Which instinct do you trust? There is something in the distance that I can't quite see, can't quite hear.

I need to understand this.

Do I imagine it? What makes me put one foot forward when something inside is saying, 'I'm not really sure about this'?

Another step, and my senses are in confusion, balancing the evidence.

The shadow inside me overrides logic and carries me forward.

99

Stephen Foster
film and TV cameraman, director and photographer

Patience
Objectivity
Nearness
Distance
Not Fixing
Not Judging
Not Interpreting
Not Knowing
Not Doing
Listening
Waiting
Accepting
Allowing
Presentness
Softness
Silence
Gentleness
Clarity
Craziness

Amazement
Wonder
Love
Kindness
Disappearance
Reappearance
Vision
Sense
Phrasing
Rhythm
Form
Pattern
Perception
Play
Music
Poetry
Darkness
Luminosity
Compassion

Sondra Horton Fraleigh
founder and director Eastwest Somatics Institute

When my mother met my father at a piano bar in Brooklyn in 1947, she made him promise to take her around the world. He got her as far as Istanbul, where they've lived for fifty years. Most of the friends with whom they explored the Mediterranean are dead now. When life without them seems too sad to bear, they console themselves with a candlelit supper at which they toast the great capitals they've yet to visit. Since time is short, their list is, too. They just want to see the cities that will astound them with their beauty.

For my parents the story is only ever just beginning...

Maureen Freely
novelist and translator

I wish I had told my parents before it was too late how proud I was of them and the way they put boundaries into place to stop us going off the tracks.

As I make my swooping last journey upwards I will get that chance and say thankyou to God for the gift of life in my grandchildren.

Our lives are full of friends that we sometimes take for granted.

'Thankyou' is the word that is always on the tip of my tongue; it's a small word but if I only had enough breath for three words they would be 'thankyou for life'.

Elaine Gaston
welfare funerals officer

It was just too beautiful to be indoors! I had to let my Lebenslust out and run across the peninsula, the sweat freezing instantly (at -24°C), my eyelashes clogging into tiny icicles. I was listening to some wild music until the batteries stopped in the cold. The abrupt silence was enhanced by creaking icefloes floating by on the water current, and a grunting Weddell seal lolling on the gravel beach. A silence so profound, it was cosmic – I wanted to store this peaceful moment away in a pocket of my mind, to call on when life is crowded.

99

Gudrun Gaudian
marine ecologist

JOINT DEFENCE TREATY

Sky
is mute

with the memory
of birds.

TEAHOUSE IN UTANO

To make a thing so small
it can never be exploded
or reduced.

Lines shorten,
thought compresses,
syntax poised

and ready.

Nouns on full alert,
each verb mindful
of its weight,

its origin.

43

Gary Geddes
poet

So brief and so bright.
Once I said no out of fear; better
say yes to everything,
yes, than miss out. Thanks
for my luck – my beloveds, my
free education, friends –
health (so far)
on this clear September day
as the wind is shaking
the long-stalked anemones,
last creamy passion-flowers
of the year,
a sharp bold robin
staring.
I've travelled the planet we live on
above the clouds, seen red sun rising

I am flying, Egypt, flying –

carry
my parents' love and lives
inside me, and now
am still here, yes here. Look, near the edge of the shadow.

Maggie Gee
novelist

February: look out for wintersweet flowers in the
front garden, next to the strawberry tree, with its
little birds including goldfinches (however did
those heads evolve?). Southwards, this year find
the old *prunus autumnalis* full of delicate pink
blossom, in flounces. Its neighbour the myrtle tree
is still laden with fruit. Some days a misselthrush
takes it over, terrorizing the blackbirds. At the
back – you have to go through the gate – a
carmine *hamamelis* is like a piece of sculpture,
flanked by slate hellebores and the red seed heads
and gleaming leaves of *iris foetidissima*. Mind the
snowdrops underfoot.

99   I tried imagining the August garden, since that is
often the peak – but my memory was too vague.
So what I have done is imagine a February garden
visitor. Everything I refer to is doing its stuff as
I describe – but an actual visitor would probably
see all the dead leaves that need clearing up, and
the pruning that needs doing. So in a way it is all
imagination. A way of cheering oneself up in this
endless winter, the secret life of gardens that no
garden visitor ever sees.

Lucy Gent
'interests include gardens and sometimes writing about them'

People behave the way they are treated. If we want respect, we must show it – no matter what the differences. Working with people on both sides of the criminal justice system, I have never been threatened or harmed. I treat convicted offenders with the same respect as judges, prison officers and police. Young offenders have been the biggest challenge. Their violence is often about demanding respect. But I treat them as potential friends, with qualities I value in my own children. I want them to respect me too. And so far they have.

Roger Graef
film-maker and criminologist

I hear the backing truck at noon,
The grub-locating pecker's thuck,
The seal's midnight, shrill, salt howl,
The Air France jet, the prowling hog,
And you wondered on the trail to Camp Pleasant,
'If a tree falls in the forest and there's no one
There to hear it, does it fall?'
The river was only sometimes loud.
I wonder if post-death there's sound.
I hear my heart in its nest,
And must say right now I've loved you
Long with a love more
Raucous than the rest, and will immediately ask
Your question, dear, silently, of God.

97

David Guterson
novelist

Buckminster Fuller's life's work explored synergy:
the structures and principles that emerge spontaneously
as things are brought together:

'Synergy is one
Of those generalized principles.
It is defined scientifically
As behaviour of whole systems
Unpredicted by behaviours
Of any of their separate parts.'

Synergy creates unexpected possibilities as things become
more complex. Gravitational attraction appears only
between two or more masses. Soft carbon added to iron
creates a much stronger more useful material – steel.
Love itself might be a prime example of synergy:

'Love
Is omni inclusive
Progressively exquisite
Understanding and tender
And compassionately attuned
To other than self.'

Jonathan Hare
scientist

SOLSTICE PADDLE

We were there at the mouth of the windblown channel
Near the end of a paddle
And the sky was opening up just as it was closing down
And Kokohead stood in a warrior cape of mist above us,
And below the boat rolled the blue kingdom of knowledge.
We paused there at the culmination of ten thousand paths:
six travelers pulling together in that sacred outrigger.
    As the day lay down behind the crater,
And one year floated up behind another
And all the births, partings and deaths we carried with us
Grew wise, then lighter.

Joy Harjo
poet, musician, performer, playwright
'who lives in Albuquerque and misses the ocean'

'Alone and blind and endlessly voyaging,' said the head of Orpheus, 'I think constantly of fidelity. Fidelity is a matter of perception; nobody is unfaithful to the sea or to mountains or to death: once recognised they fill the heart. In love or in terror or in loathing one responds to them with the true self; fidelity is not an act of the will: the soul is compelled by recognitions. Anyone who loves, anyone who perceives the other person fully can only be faithful, can never be unfaithful to the sea and the mountains and the death in that person, so pitiable and heroic is it to be a human being.'

111

Russell Hoban sent this 111-word excerpt from his 1987 novel *The Medusa Frequency*. When I pointed out that 99 was the crucial number, he responded with an 89-word version of the same piece – but I missed every word he had omitted. So he suggested that I award him a 12-word voucher against a contribution of less than 99 – which I gave him on the arrival of Sondra Horton Fraleigh's 43 words.

Hoban has changed one word from the original version in the last line of the piece – it has taken him 18 years, he says, to be able to make this change from 'pitiful' to 'pitiable'. LG

Russell Hoban
novelist

AUGUST 6, AND AGAIN ON AUGUST 9

People on the far shore
slid rows of lanterns upon the water,
nudged them

      go   go   go

Paper and tiny flames shook
     no no   no no

We willed them (replicas of lives) –
Blow downstream toward the setting sun.
But wind breathed them
to our side of the water,
where nodding, turning,
they shyly touched
one another.

'There's mine!'
A little girl sees her writing:

>No More Bombs
>On Hiroshima
>On Nagasaki
>On Iraq
>On NY City

A loudspeaker
calls. 'Jonathan,
your mother's looking for you.'
A man in a wheelchair zooms across
the bridge, sailing an American flag.

99

Maxine Hong Kingston
writer and poet

Resilience can only be attained by coming through adversity.

To truly get over something, you have to go through it – but when we do, we can be better human beings for it. More understanding, more compassionate, more insightful –

a life lived with more purpose.

Embracing and understanding mental or physical pain can bring us closer to our authentic selves. From there we can recycle that experience into helping others which in turn nurtures our soul.

For a better world – strive to live authentically, flex the gifts you have been given,

live with love and laugh wherever possible.

Matthew Johnstone
author and illustrator

The last lines of *The Origin of Species* are inspiring, hopeful, and precise.

'Thus, from the war of nature, from famine and death, the most exalted object which we are capable of conceiving, namely, the production of the higher animals, directly follows. There is grandeur in this view of life, with its several powers, having been originally breathed into a few forms or into one; and that, whilst this planet has gone cycling on according to the fixed law of gravity, from so simple a beginning endless forms most beautiful and most wonderful have been, and are being, evolved.'

Charles Darwin

Steve Jones
geneticist

Above all try to be kind. I have no doubt kindness is the greatest virtue. You can find a million reasons in any one day to dislike people, to feel resentment or even loathing. But to be kind is to protect yourself from the worst parts of your own nature. You may fear that to face people with an open heart leaves you vulnerable, open to abuse. I rather doubt it. The way of the hard face is much harder. Be kind to others, especially the more difficult people you encounter, and that kindness will come back to you.

Fergal Keane
journalist, writer, broadcaster

Happiness isn't for tomorrow.
It's not hypothetical,
it starts here and now.
Down with violence, egoism
and despair, stop pessimism.
Let's pick ourselves up.
Nature has given us
extraordinary things.
It's not over yet, nothing is decided.

Intelligently, in our own way,
at our own rhythm,
like responsible men proud of their inheritance,
let's build the country of our children
and stop taking pity on ourselves.
Africa is also the joy of living,
optimism, beauty, elegance,
grace, poetry, softness, the sun,
and nature.
Let's be happy to be its sons
and fight to build our happiness.

Salif Keita
singer and songwriter

Don't waste time. If you've got something useful to do, get on with it.

At 21, anyone of 30 was over the hump. At 30, 50-year-olds had a foot in the grave. At 50, old people were 70 plus. Now between 80 and 85, I want to know where the years went.

Even young women stand up and give me a seat on the Tube. How did it all go so fast? Moral: don't waste life. It's too wonderful, interesting and challenging for that. But will God manage down here without me when I've gone?

Bruce Kent
peace campaigner, honorary vice-president
Campaign for Nuclear Disarmament

I have been working with people with dementia for over
sixteen years, transcribing their words and shaping their poems.

NEAR NATURE

One lady said to me, 'We're a nice little two-lot, you and me. I like
us being with us.' This is a better description of relationship than
I have managed. Another lady said, 'I bet you've never been so near
Nature before.' She was right: the gift of dementia to the rest of
us is to enable us to see more clearly that what is most important
is not intellectual development but emotional depth and honesty.

79

John Killick
poet and writer

Hey Jules, it's Brian

                    I'm on a plane and it's hijacked

    It doesn't look good

Live your life the best you can, and

           know that I love you and, no matter what,

    I'll see you again.

Honey

          something terrible

    is happening   I don't think

          I'm going to make it

    I love you.

Laurie, I love you

I'm in the Trade Center

The building was hit by something

I don't know

if I'm going to get out.

Lyzbeth, I love you a thousand times   I need you

to be happy.

Mommy, the building is on fire

I love you, Mommy.

99   Here is my 99-word piece. My colleague who is a poet,
Janet R Kirchheimer, and I talked about the essay I was trying
to write and nothing gelled until we listened to my chant of the
final conversations from September 11. The melody is taken
from the chanting of the biblical book of Lamentations traditionally
read on the day when the destruction of the Temple in Jerusalem
is remembered. Janet and I worked together to transform this
song into a poem.

Irwin Kula
rabbi and writer, president Clal,
the National Jewish Center for Learning and Leadership, New York

After working with Irwin Kula on his poem,
Janet Kirchheimer sent one of her own. LG

ASHES

Each day, Bill Butler comes,
searching for his son,
 'Where are you, boy?'
each day, ten hours,
one hundred and eighteen days
so far,
searching rubble that goes sixty feet below the earth
to bring his son home, bury him.

Where I search, there is no rubble,
only different layers of ash, bits of scattered bone,
 'Where are you, Oma,
near the barbed wire, ovens, chimneys?'
One day she came to me, told me to stop looking,
 'I'm not there anymore. I've escaped
into the air, into particles so small they can no longer
be seen by the living.'

99

Janet R Kirchheimer
poet and teaching fellow, Clal

Design reflects the preoccupations of every era –
the Victorians romanticised the past and endeavoured,
often with considerable success, to incorporate
technological advance within historicist structures.
Moderns, like Le Corbusier, strove for rationality and
tried to transform society. Sometimes this worked but
tower blocks, a modernist legacy, were not the answer
to urban living. Ultimately, order transcends the manners
of the times and individual cultures. Minimalism can
be seen, however, not so much as an affectation, but as
a form of politeness and discretion. Eras pass swiftly.
Lack of pomposity and affectation and, above all,
modesty, characterise the best design.

99

Alastair Lansley
architect, leader of design and reconstruction, St Pancras Station, London

FUTUROLOGY

I cannot break free from these iron stars.
I want the raspberry paw-pads of the fox,
but here are only claws, the Crab, the Scorpion.
Great shining signs that slide across the sky.

I want the wisdom ignorant of wars
and the soft key that opens all the locks.
I want the touch of fur, the slant of sun
deep in a golden, slotted, changing eye.

O let there be no signs! Let fall the bars,
and walls be moss-grown, scattered rocks.
Let all the evil we have done be done
and minds lie still as sunlit meadows lie.

99   I have a slightly woo-woo story to tell you.
I wasn't at all sure I wanted to take the
proposal seriously but as soon as I considered
what I could contribute, a recent poem that
might fit the 'If you had breath for just 99
words' thing came into my head. And it stuck
there, till I had to say come on, stupid, that
poem won't be exactly 99 words long. Then
of course I had to go count it. And it was.

I feel like an Augur or something.

Ursula K Le Guin
novelist and poet

There is a grace approaching
that we shun as much as death,
it is the completion of our birth.

It does not come in time,
    but in timelessness
when the mind sinks into the heart
and we remember.

It is an insistent grace that draws us
to the edge and beckons us surrender
safe territory and enter our enormity.

We know we must pass
    beyond knowing
and fear the shedding.

Pulled by our homesickness
through forgotten ghosts
    and unexpected angels
there is nothing left to say
but we are That.

And That is what we sing about.

Stephen Levine
poet, writer and teacher

THE APPLE PIP

Small as an apple pip, they say,
my daughter's baby sleeps and dreams
and from the wool of sleep now draws
the new thread of a thin-spun life,
from clouds that catch among the stars,
from ripples in the blood's dark streams,
from breath and rain, from north and south.

With apples once I wooed my love
and now love plants another root
and unexpected pulls the quiet
around that tiny knot of life,
the seed a growing labyrinth,
the child within the girl who lies
curled in her bed within the room
within the house, within the house.

99

Grevel Lindop
poet and travel writer

I dreamt one day of surrounding the world
with joy. A chain of Andrew Logan Museums
of Sculpture in every continent with a message
of celebration of man's existence on this planet.
Even as a young man I wanted to help humanity
in my best way. Window cleaning, giving parties
and making beautiful things. This has been my
path. A few tips – be kind to your fellow human
beings – never give up – take care of the earth
and all the creatures that inhabit its surface.

Birth – a surprise
Life – a privilege
Death – a new door

Embrace the moment. Smile.

Andrew Logan
sculptor, stage and festival designer

GOOD MEMORIES
TO A ROTTING SHEEP TO VIOLET FLOWERS TO AN OAK TREE
TO AVON HEAD TO A SMALL STONE
TO MISSISSIPPI RIVER BLUES TO ROLLING THUNDER TO A FLY IN THE EYE
TO NAKER'S HILL IN A SQUALL TO PLYM HEAD
TO SHEEP'S TOR TO BLUEBELLS TO BELLOWING CATTLE TO WHITE BLOSSOM
TO A FARMYARD TO A BROWN BULL
TO DARTMEET TO COFFIN STONE TO CAWING TO HAMELDOWN CAIRN
TO A STRAND OF WOOL TO THE SMELL OF NEW BRACKEN TO MOTIONLESS
TO PINE NEEDLES
TO STEPPING-STONES TO HUCCABY RING TO LAUGHTER TOR
TO GOOD FEELINGS

from *A DARTMOOR WALK, eight days in England,* 1987

Richard Long
sculptor and land artist

Peace is a long time coming,
Peace is my prayer for this earth.
More and more blood is shed on this earth,
Famine is everywhere, and life is getting harder.

Let's wake up, all as one, and do something before it's too late.

Bloodshed spreads, famine increases.
Sons of the earth rise up all as one to prevent this before it's too late.

Life is getting harder on earth
Bloodshed spreads and hunger is upon us.

Late in the night, the stars sparkle above,
I wake up suddenly,
I cannot sleep,
So much am I suffering for humanity.

Baaba Maal
musician and UNDP Youth Emissary

Dear Liz, I wonder whether this, a version in fact of the last words of my first book, about mountains, might suit. It suddenly seemed that they might, because they are obliquely about death in life, but explicitly about the value of life, and living, and going on living, and the love of being in a place at a time.

That day on the mountain-top, within the falling snow, I didn't feel cocooned by the snow but extended by it: part of the great realm of land over which the snow was falling. My mind moved east, to where snow fell upon the ancient granite of the Cairngorms. It moved north, to where snow fell upon the wilderness of the grey Monadhliaths. It moved west, to where snow fell upon The Rough Bounds of Knoydart. I thought of the snow falling across ridges of invisible hills, and I thought that there was nowhere I would rather be than there.

Robert Macfarlane
writer

If the Lord looks at you, let it be with my eyes.

And if I look at you, let it be with your eyes.

And if your eyes look at me, let them look and find fault with the Lord for letting me look with your eyes.

If my eyes look at the Lord, let them see him for what he is.

What he is is your eyes looking at my eyes, seeing you in them, them in you.

You are what I see when the Lord looks at me, and I do not believe in the Lord.

Frank McGuinness
poet and playwright

It is never my custom to use words lightly.
If twenty-seven years in prison have done anything
to us, it was to use the silence of solitude to make
us understand how precious words are and how
real speech is in its impact on the way people live
and die.

From the introduction to the closing address
at the xiii International Aids Conference,
Durban, South Africa, 14 July, 2000.

50

Nelson Mandela
first democratically elected President of South Africa

The United States should join all nations in dismantling institutions that inflict retribution and instead take actions that foster reconciliation. Capital punishment is an instrument of retribution that deepens social divisions. Each execution denies the humanity of its victim by extinguishing the most basic human right: existence. Abolishing capital punishment would help bridge the social fault lines that separate us and generate fear and insecurity. We will reaffirm our common humanity when all governments refuse to carry out socially sanctioned, cold-blooded, ritualized killings. This is how the universal abolition of capital punishment will foster a safer, more secure world.

99

Robert Meeropol
attorney, activist, writer, founder and executive director
Rosenberg Fund for Children

Imagination is the key. It enables us to take on any form: Egyptian goddess, Scottish housewife, Macuxi warrior, demon, frog or cartoon rabbit. According to Darwin, we were all fish once anyway. Imagination is effortlessly trans-national, trans-racial, trans-gender and trans-species. There is a shuttle service between the imagination and the real world. They influence each other. We can imagine things that are not and bring them about. For that reason and in the name of flux, shuttle and transformation, I take as my tutelary spirits Legba and Hermes, the trickster gods of gateways, boundaries, borders and communication – thieves too.

Pauline Melville
actress and writer

PEACETIME HAIKU

Try one hundred years
without any wars at all –
let's see if it works!

Adrian Mitchell
poet, novelist and playwright

Bones are people. This is how the Huguenot refugees, master craftsmen and journeymen weavers of Spitalfields live again 200 years after they were buried. So too do the Neolithic people of Çatalhüyük, Anatolia. Their bones tell how they wrecked their health living in dark, smoky rooms – a recipe for emphysema in old age. Yet they hunted the great bull, sculpted the tiny headless figurine and ground the ochre, capturing on the walls inside their homes the raindrops falling on the parched lake outside. Across 10,000 years, bones are a way to pass on our stories.

Theya Molleson
anthropologist

The Prophet said in a hadith that God has 99
names, 100 minus 1. Whoever enumerates them will
enter Paradise. But why 99? The answer came to me
unexpectedly.

If we take a regular cube 10x10x10 units and we
open it this way, 1 of the 100 inner cubes remains
uncovered – perhaps the 100 minus 1 to which the
Prophet referred.

Mathematics illustrates here how unity of
the main cube produces infinite multiplicity.
The Qu'ran states that God made the cube a
symbol of Divine Oneness for mankind. God is
One but His Attributes are endless octaves of 99.

99

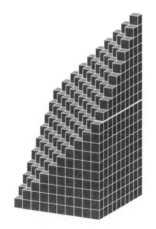

Ahmed Moustafa
calligrapher and artist

'A universe simple enough to be understood is too simple to produce a mind capable of understanding it.'

John D Barrow, physicist

If we learned that a butterfly was getting ulcers worrying about the universe, we would attempt to console her by explaining how limited her knowledge was. But aren't we in the same boat? 150 years ago we did not know about the existence of atoms, or of distant galaxies. Think of what remains to be discovered. And yet we wonder, and worry. Wonder and worry are as gloriously characteristic of us as the markings on the butterfly's wings.

99

Walter Murch
film editor and sound designer

Living gratefully on stolen time, I reflect on the meaning of my classical existence. I have assisted in the rebirth of that great eighteenth century idea, the Republic of Letters. Everywhere young people, as in the Middle Ages, speak two languages, their birth language and the new universal language of English, which shares with the old universal language of Latin the merit of possessing a great literature; along with Greek they are the key to European culture. The spontaneous movement of populations has broken the old ethnic boundaries, and will eventually create the ancient Stoic dream of world citizenship.

99

99 words, that's a tall order (since famous last words are usually much shorter). But I'm happy to make a try. In fact I feel rather in tune having been told a year ago that I had a 25% chance of dropping dead within the year.

Oswyn Murray
classicist

'When you know what you are doing, you can do what you want.'

Moshe Feldenkrais (1904–1984)

How to know what you are doing?
- go slowly so as to feel more clearly
- engage your senses in all you do – look, listen, taste, feel
- learn to recognize when you are making unnecessary efforts
- make the process more important than the achievement of the goal
- discover new possibilities beyond the habitual
- pay attention to the movement of your breath
- find your way, not one that others have prescribed for you
- balance flexibility with stability; activity with stillness
- explore new movements!

Garet Newell
director, Feldenkrais International Training Centre

Matthew 5

Then he taught, saying:
Blessed are the poor in spirit, the kingdom of heaven is theirs.
Blessed are those who mourn, they shall be consoled.
Blessed are the gentle, they shall inherit the land.
Blessed are those who hunger and thirst for justice, the justice
    of God shall be theirs.
Blessed are the merciful, mercy shall be shown unto them.
Blessed are the pure of heart, they shall behold their God.
Blessed are those who bring peace, they shall be children of God.
Blessed are those who suffer in the cause of right, the kingdom of
    heaven is theirs.

99

Nóirín Ní Riain
singer, teacher, scholar of plainchant and Celtic song

There is an old dog slowly dying in this house, and I am absorbed in his going. He's a tired old boy now and his thin flanks shiver with palsy. But he lies quietly, looking at the wall, and I call what I see in his milky old eyes patience and acceptance.

Let me learn from you again! I whisper to him. Let me know how to die as you do!

He makes a gentle movement with his floppy tail to send me loving greetings from wherever he is in his head.

He was always a most courteous dog.

Nuala O'Faolain
journalist, writer

I hope this is suitable. I always use the small 'i'
rather than a capital 'I' when referring to myself.
Beannachtaí Peadar

i became, of many generations, on a green island.
A form of energy called human, i am complete when i
exist simultaneously, equally balanced, in three different
dimensions – material, spiritual and creative. It is part
of my condition that achieving this balance is extremely
difficult and the struggle to achieve it consumes my time.

My time exists between my past and future – the 'now'.

A feeling or emotion called love drives the combustion
of this energy and is common to all three dimensions even
though the dimensions are separate from each other.

In the now, love is all.

98

Peadar Ó Riada
musician and composer

肉体に受けた傷や肉体に生じた傷は、やがてかさぶたとなり、傷は癒されてゆきます。内的な心に受けた傷は、これをしっかりと受けとめ堪え忍ぶことによって、その体験の中にいつしか歓びと悲しみが生じ、やがて言葉では語り得ない、肉体を通してのみ表現されるポエジィの世界へと到達する、と私は思っています。

Our bodily wounds eventually close and heal, but there are always hidden wounds, those of the heart and if you know how to accept and endure them you will discover the pain and joy which is impossible to express with words. You will reach the realm of poetry which only the body can express.

Kazuo Ohno 大野一雄
Butoh dancer and teacher

Tomorrow's music sleeps
in undiscovered orchestras,
in unmade violins,
in coiled strings.
Spring waits by the lakes,
listening to the unfurling daffodils.
Summer lingers with the
hyperborean worms,
awaiting an astonishing command
from the all-seeing eye of Ra.
Tomorrow's music sleeps
in our fingers,
in our awakening souls,
the blossom of our spirit,
the suggestive buds of our hearts.
Tell everyone the idea
is to function together
as good musicians would
in undefined future orchestras.

from *Lines in Potentis*

Ben Okri
poet and novelist

If one billion people in the world think peace – we'll get peace.
You may think 'how are we going to get one billion people
    to think PEACE?'
Remember, each one of us has the power to change the world.
Power works in mysterious ways.
Visualize the domino effect, and just start thinking PEACE.
Thoughts are infectious.
Send it out.
The message will circulate faster than you think.
It's time for action.
The action is PEACE.
Spread the WORD.
Spread PEACE.

yoko ono, summer of 2004

Yoko Ono
artist, musician and peace campaigner

I held my mother's hand as she lay dying
And felt something moving, at last, in my heart.
It was so slow and yet time was flying,
It was the end and the time to start.
As she faded I was longing to be heard;
It was stronger than familiar skin, roses or snow
This desire to find the only, the perfect word.
I tried to explain and she said: I know.
I washed her, saying, I love you so much.
I love you so much. She said it too.
Soon after that, silence, and the language of touch.

Sally Potter
film-maker

Why should I worry about dying?
I'm in heaven already
Do you not see?
For I spend all my time
On my loved river
In a beautiful town by the sea
Where my maker is always
With me
Be they a he or a she
And an angel sits
On my gunnels
Just to look out for me
From when the sun
Comes up in the morning
To when the phases of the moon
Draw up the height of the sea
I have lived luckier than anyone
So what right have I to protest
When my maker calls me?

Kevin Pyne
poet and boatman

'I was here'; from Lascaux to Banksy, from the Pyramids to Mt Rushmore the desire to leave a mark seems ubiquitous. We rail against eternity, as if time could be frozen, like Canute unable to stem the inevitable tide of process and metamorphosis.

What arrogance, what futility.

And yet; making a mark somehow verifies and makes tangible our sense of being, our singularity, our consciousness. The act of making reassures us of our very existence and in doing so heals our solitude and loneliness. To know the world and to be known by it in an almost biblical sense.

Peter Randall-Page
sculptor

D H Lawrence wrote: 'I am part of the Sun as my eye is part of me. That I am part of the Earth my feet know perfectly, and my blood is part of the sea.' This poetic vision of nature's unity resonates well with modern science. We share common ancestry with every creature on Earth. Our constituent atoms were forged in ancient stars. We live – transiting briefly from dust to dust – on a 'pale blue dot' in a vast Galaxy. But we're linked into a 'cosmic web'. In Charles Darwin's words, 'There is grandeur in this view of life'.

Martin Rees
cosmologist and astrophysicist, Astronomer Royal

NOW AND THEN

May I listen, Beloved,
May I hear,
May I feel You-So-Near ...
Closer than breath
Or ground beneath.

Pulsing red like blood
In dark body of earth,
Blinking like scintillating
Star-eyes in delight ...

May I listen, Beloved,
May I hear,
O Invisible One ...
Your gentle Breathing
Should mine fail.

Melanie Reinhart
astrologer and writer

'Will you still need me, will you still feed me, when I'm 64?'

Why, of all numbers, this? Because it's the last time anyone will re-double, double up, whether in laughter or in pain. 1 becomes 2 becomes 4 becomes 8 becomes 16 becomes 32 becomes 64. And then? Not 128, not even for 'the ninety and nine just persons' of whom the parable speaks.

'And age, and then the only end of age' (Larkin). 'Most things may never happen: this one will' (Larkin, harping). 'Your days are numbered, so are mine' (Bob Dylan, the person with the harp).

99

Christopher Ricks
'CR teaches at Boston University'

Raised by a single mother I spent my childhood discovering my imagination. Solitude was incessant but I was never alone. I had over 20 friends.

I played with the letters of the alphabet the way most girls play with dolls. I assigned a colour to each. 'E' was yellow, 'r' brown, 'a' azure. They talked, danced, quarrelled.

I never tired of this game. Changing meanings by shuffling letters is pure magic. Words shimmy, laugh. When they are censured they bleed. I nurse them, the way I would my own flesh. For I know, deep inside, that words are alive.

Elif Shafak
novelist and journalist

tar	peg	ego	pen	dog
hum	ask	git	pin	nog
rum	gam	era	ebb	fee
wet	dot	gob	son	coo
elm	jab	awe	fen	new
log	hug	nil	hop	wig
cud	hun	gad	ate	gig
ken	due	bay	aye	how
bat	wot	jay	sea	cig
mix	ark	tom	yam	jut
lug	hat	auk	jug	shy
gin	can	gip	nit	dig
fog	bet	ten	jib	end
cub	fee	fez	cot	fem

gem	fad	sky	pry	key
elk	fie	gun	tux	asp
gas	pod	tie	ant	ram
say	web	cod	alp	leg
jot	use	tad	beg	she
act	axe	way	fir	

Here is my contribution. I have no idea whether you will like it or understand it – there may be an aspergerish component to my personality that this appeals to. But while I was 'collecting' these random words, I had a wonderful appreciation of the long history of the English language, as I saw 'ken' and 'wot' and 'gam' and 'fem', and all the others. Anyway, I don't blame you if you think it's too weird, but as I typed over this list, I got the same sort of pleasure that I got when I was seeing the words – objects and associations leaping out at me from even the most random encounters with language.

Jane Smiley
novelist

Stay true to the voice within. This voice beckons us
at birth and bids us be unafraid of death. It knows
what is right and never bends to fear. It informs our
finest thinking and boldest decisions. It is in tune
with nature and the things of the spirit. It speaks the
truth when lies assail us. It strengthens and softens
our loving. It encourages creation, play, laughter. It
whispers reminders of our humanity. It confirms our
place in the scheme of things. It celebrates our right
choices. It knows us well. It is the guide we can trust.

99

Christopher Spence
counsellor and writer, founder director London Lighthouse,
former chief executive Volunteering England

Life is so much simpler than people make it out to be. With respect to any serious decision, does your proposal take us closer to our ideal society? If so, do it. If not, don't. Then stop worrying and go play cricket unless, of course, your bizarre notion of Utopia does not include such pleasures...

Clive Stafford Smith
director UK charity Reprieve, representing prisoners on death row
and held in secret prisons beyond the rule of law

Why would I waste my breath?

Elizabeth St John
movement and healing practitioner

What we know is ringed with darkness; God, however, sees it as light. Find the courage to trust this Reality; remember God every day. Strive to embrace all creation. If we are with God when all is well, He will be with us when life wounds. Seek what exalts you, and live 'à toutes risques'. Life is a dream, but it is not our dream. All that happens to you is sent from God. Aspire to that state of bliss which inhabits all things. For 'God is a beautiful being, and He loves beauty.' Your true Self is God.

99

John Tavener
musician and composer

Ubuntu is very difficult to render into a Western language. It speaks of the very essence of being human. When we want to give high praise to someone we say, 'Yu, u nobuntu'; 'Hey, he or she has ubuntu.' This means they are generous, hospitable, friendly, caring and compassionate. They share what they have. It also means my humanity is caught up, is inextricably bound up, in theirs. We belong in a bundle of life... It is not 'I think therefore I am'. It says rather: 'I am human because I belong.' I participate, I share.

from *No Future without Forgiveness*

Desmond Tutu
Archbishop Emeritus of Cape Town, human rights, peace and reconciliation advocate

You do not need to leave your room.
Remain sitting at your table and listen.
Do not even listen,
Simply wait.
Do not even wait,
Simply be quite still and solitary.
The world will freely offer itself to you to
    be unmasked.
It has no choice.
It will roll in ecstasy at your feet.

Franz Kafka

Harry Underhill
mediator, hydrologist, Quaker

'Good morning,' said the little prince.

'Good morning,' said the shopkeeper.

His shop sold pills which were guaranteed to quench your thirst. You take one a week and need never drink again.

'Why are you selling those?' asked the little prince.

'They save a lot of time,' said the shopkeeper. 'Experts have worked out that they save fifty-three minutes a week.'

'And what do people do with their fifty-three minutes?'

'Anything they want.'

'If I had fifty-three minutes to spare,' said the little prince, 'I'd take a stroll down to the fountain...'

from *The Little Prince*, by Antoine de Saint-Exupéry, translated by Alan Wakeman.

– Bonjour, dit le petit prince.

– Bonjour, dit le marchand.

C'était un marchand de pilules perfectionneés qui apaisent la soif. On en avale une par semain et l'on n'éprouve plus besoin de boire.

– Pourquoi vends-tu ça? dit le petit prince.

– C'est une grosse économie de temps, dit le marchand. Les experts ont fait des calculs. On épargne cinquante-trois minutes par semaine.

– Et que fait-on de ces cinquante-trois minutes?

– On en fait ce que l'on veut.

«Moi, se dit le petit prince, si j'avais cinquante-trois minutes à dépenser, je marcherais tout doucement vers une fontaine...»

Alan Wakeman
poet and translator of Saint-Exupéry

The principle of rhythm explains the cycles of life, the truth that everything has a tide-like ebb and flow... People are born, grow, meet their demise, and like the phoenix are reborn. We can see rhythm manifested plainly in the seasons. Spring is the birth or beginning, summer is the period of maturation and constancy, and fall is the encroaching ebb or decline, which ushers in winter, the season of death; with the passing of winter, there is rebirth in the spring.

One lesson of this law is that there is no absolute rest, no cessation from rhythm's cycle.

from *Ancient Future* by Wayne B Chandler

Randy Weston
jazz pianist and composer

So this is the end – and I hope it IS the end.

Heaven and hell? Not sure where I'd end up.

Reincarnation? Terrifying; I've been so lucky in this life – finding exactly the right work and exactly the right man; I could hardly hope to do so well again.

Remember the tale of the guru telling his proud emperor, as they watched a line of ants crossing their terrace, 'Every one of those ants once had an empire bigger than yours'? I'd far prefer A E Housman's

'Goodnight; ensured release
Imperishable peace,
Have these for yours,'

Have these for mine.

Katharine Whitehorn
journalist and writer

And maybe ninety-nine times *Love* should be
the simplest last expression of all of us sounding
out the sole syllable of human essence and
saying within it the sum of our experience, of
our lifetime's knowledge of what great or small
kindness, what desire, forgiveness, understanding
and acceptance we received or gave or felt, and
in saying *Love* so know our own failures and that
these were loved too and forgiven too and so on
one last breath tentatively venture all yearning and
gratitude letting the sound travel in the hopelessly
enduring hope of its somewhere being heard:
Love.

Niall Williams
novelist and playwright

We in Westminster live in an instant world. Dramatic events surround us, often one piece of breaking news succeeds another like the waves of the sea. Digital clocks urge us to hurry. Yet time, like music, should unroll slowly. We age gradually, wrinkle by wrinkle. Our seasons are subtle, spring edges in as flowers bud and leaves uncurl. Autumn comes slowly, celebrating and mourning the advance of each year.

It provides a lesson for politics. Human problems take time to resolve. Human hearts (and minds) build trust slowly. There are few instant fixes. Patience is the mark of statesmanship.

99

Shirley Williams
former Liberal Democrat leader of the House of Lords

Silence is a place we all inhabit, but about which
not enough is said. Silence is never equivalent
to the complete absence of sound or of meaning.
We all know that the space of silence is delineated
according to certain arbitrary but powerfully
reinforced conventions, rarely violated. What we
hear every day in a host of ways is focused, directed
and purposeful silence, based on the notion that
there is a difference between the sayable and the
unsayable, and that such a distinction could and
should be maintained and observed over time.
Our non-speech acts define who we are.

Jay Winter
historian

Have you ever wanted to throw yourself off the roof of your own life? As the quickest exit to elsewhere? But there was no elsewhere; it was here. This blue planet spun in stars. We were lucky; we had a whole life and we stretched it as far as it could go. A life-line. A tightrope. What is my life? A rope slung across space. And I spent it telling stories because a story is a tightrope between two worlds. Thank you for taking a walk with me. Thank you for everything. Love is the last word. Love.

Jeanette Winterson
novelist

As dusk descends on the city park, the swings fall still, the noise from the paddling pool fades, the picnic rugs are folded, the dog-walkers make one last circuit, and the tennis players and footballers move towards the pub, or supper. Lovers entwined beneath the chestnut trees brush the grass from their clothes and leave.

The pleasures of parks are to be had for free: a counter-world to what Henry Miller called the air-conditioned nightmare. They offer a vision of a more convivial form of society, the ethical basis for anything that wants to call itself the green revolution.

Ken Worpole
writer and environmentalist

'To walk by faith is to construct a beautiful dream and live it.' LW

The greatest gifts of the human experience belonged to us as children: a sense of wonder, curiosity and determination. Later, we experienced culture, ideals, and the expectations of modern society. Yet, how many rules and beliefs have become pieces of our identity?

Set the world back a pace. Remember to play, make yourself laugh, hang upside down, ask all kinds of questions, be irreverent and seek adventure. Reclaiming these gifts is like remembering a dream. Remember and then make up the parts that you've forgotten. Being authentic, living for the sake of life itself, is an act of faith.

Lizz Wright
jazz singer and songwriter

'In the beginning was the Word.' But how can that be? Like, 'In our beginning was the Boot'? Feet were designed to fit into Boots? I don't think so! As Ira Gershwin wrote, 'Things that you're liable to read in the bible... ain't necessarily so.'

Language can hide what it pretends to represent. What are extremists/Indians/Vizigoths/ Travellers? People. More like you and me than not. And what are people? Animals. And so on.

Strip away words as clothes. Reveal the shockingly vulnerable intimacy of the universe.

Then start again. Next time, hopefully, not just dressed to kill.

PS To be honest, if I only had say 10 minutes to live (9.9?) I'd like to apologise to anyone I'd ever hurt

Robert Wyatt
musician

In the past, stone was used to tell stories, to let people know about Gods and Queens and Princes, athletes and victors, the famous and the glorious, the vanquished and the foes. Stone was the best material to serve man's grandest ambitions. I can't really do that. I don't want to make the stone my servant: a bigger wilder story is told by the stone itself, of the earth, and the universe. Perhaps I use the human form to let the people see the stone, so it can tell its story, which is part of my story, our story.

Emily Young
sculptor

The world is filled with people who do not say
what they think, either from politeness, or fear,
or hypocrisy, or uncertainty about their beliefs.
The search for freedom of speech has barely begun,
and we are still surrounded by a great darkness
of hidden thoughts. I started the Muse to illustrate
that darkness, not just because thoughts become
lonely and limp unless fertilized by constant
interaction, but also to stimulate ways of working
that are less frustrating, and to create a place
where men and women can participate in a great
adventure, discovering how interesting other
people are.

99

Theodore Zeldin
philosopher, historian and writer

CONTRIBUTORS

Almond, David

Aridjis, Homero

Ashrawi, Hanan

Athill, Diana

Baca, Susana

Bamber, Helen

Barks, Coleman

Batchelor, Martine

Batchelor, Stephen

Batmanghelidjh, Camila

Benn, Tony

Boothroyd, Betty

Busby, Margaret

Cassidy, Sheila

Chatto, Beth

Clarke, Gillian

Collins, Grenville

Cope, Wendy

Critchlow, Keith

Dalrymple, William

Darr, Robert Abdul Hayy

Djerassi, Carl

Dorfman, Ariel

Doust, Gill

Downie, Graham

Ellams, Inua

Elworthy, Scilla

Erguner, Kudsi

Fermine, Maxence
and
Cornicard, Stéphane

Fiennes, William

Foster, Stephen

Fraleigh, Sondra Horton

Freely, Maureen

Gaston, Elaine

Gaudian, Gudrun

Geddes, Gary

Gee, Maggie

Gent, Lucy

Graef, Roger

Guterson, David

Hare, Jonathan

Harjo, Joy

Hoban, Russell

Hong Kingston, Maxine

Johnstone, Matthew

Jones, Steve

Keane, Fergal

Keita, Salif

Kent, Bruce

Killick, John

Kula, Irwin
and
Kirchheimer, Janet R

Lansley, Alastair

Le Guin, Ursula K

Levine, Stephen

Lindop, Grevel

Logan, Andrew

Long, Richard

Maal, Baaba

Macfarlane, Robert

McGuinness, Frank

Mandela, Nelson

Meeropol, Robert

Melville, Pauline

Mitchell, Adrian

Molleson, Theya

Moustafa, Ahmed

Murch, Walter

Murray, Oswyn

Newell, Garet

Ní Riain, Nóirin

O'Faolain, Nuala

Ó Riada, Peadar

Ohno, Kazuo

Okri, Ben

Ono, Yoko

Potter, Sally

Pyne, Kevin

Randall-Page, Peter

Rees, Martin

Reinhart, Melanie

Ricks, Christopher

Shafak, Elif

Smiley, Jane

Spence, Christopher

Stafford Smith, Clive

St John, Elizabeth

Tavener, John

Tutu, Desmond

Underhill, Harry

Wakeman, Alan

Weston, Randy

Whitehorn, Katharine

Williams, Niall

Williams, Shirley

Winter, Jay

Winterson, Jeanette

Worpole, Ken

Wright, Lizz

Wyatt, Robert

Young, Emily

Zeldin, Theodore

ACKNOWLEDGEMENTS

Liz Gray and Darton, Longman & Todd would like to thank the following writers and publishers for their permission to reproduce copyright material in *99 words*. Every effort has been made to trace copyright holders of the material used in this book to secure permission for reproducing it. If any required acknowledgements have been omitted, or any rights overlooked, it is unintentional and we apologize. If notified we will be happy to rectify any omissions or make any amendments necessary in future printings of this book.

Listed in the order in which the material appears.

Homero Aridjis, *Ojos de otro mirar* (México, Ediciones El Tucán de Virginia, 1998), translation by George McWhirter, *Eyes to See Otherwise/Ojos de otro mirar* (Manchester, Carcanet, 2001)

Coleman Barks, extract from *The Essential Rumi* (USA: Harper Collins, 1995)

Muhyiddin Ibn'Arabi, extract from *Fusus al-Hikam*, vol.3 (translation and commentary by Ismail Hakki Bursevi, rendered into English by Bulent Rauf (Ibn'Arabi Society, 2003)

Robert Abdul Hayy Darr, translations of Rumi, *Clarifications* (London: Archetype, 2011)

Janet R Kirchheimer, *How to Spot One of Us* (New York: Clal, 2007)

Ursula K Le Guin, 'Futurology' from *Incredible Good Fortune* (Shambhala, 2006)

Baaba Maal, 'Hunger' (Blue Mountain Music, 2002)

Kazuo Ohno, from '*My Mother: Watashi no Okaa-san*' Butoh dance programme, 1981

Ben Okri, 'Lines in Potentis' (2002) by permission of The Marsh Agency Ltd

Desmond Tutu, extract from *No Future Without Forgiveness* (London: Rider Books, 2000. Reprinted by permission of the Random House Group Ltd)

Antoine de Saint-Exupéry, translated by Alan Wakeman, extract from *The Little Prince* (London: Pavilion Books, 1997 and Paris: Librairie Gallimard, 1946)

Wayne B Chandler, extract from *Ancient Future* (Baltimore, MD: Black Classic Press, 1999)